DUŠAN PETRIČIĆ

MY TORONTO

Introduction by
Rick
Salutin

McArthur & Company
Toronto

First published in 2011 by
McArthur & Company
322 King Street West, Suite 402
Toronto, Ontario
M5V 1J2
www.mcarthur-co.com

Library and Archives Canada Cataloguing in Publication
Petričić, Dušan
My Toronto / Dušan Petričić ; introduction by Rick Salutin.

ISBN 978-1-77087-058-1

1. Toronto (Ont.)--Social life and customs--21st century--Caricatures and cartoons. 2. Petričić, Dušan. 3. Canadian wit and humor, Pictorial--Ontario--Toronto. I. Title.

FC3097.3.P48 2011 971.3'541 C2011-904322-X

The publisher would like to acknowledge the financial support of the Government of Canada through the Canada Book Fund and the Canada Council for our publishing activities. The publisher further wishes to acknowledge the financial support of the Ontario Arts Council and the OMDC for our publishing program.

Design by Jelena Reljić

Printed and bound in Canada

10 9 8 7 6 5 4 3 2 1

For Dragana,
with whom I share the thrilling process of understanding Toronto.

Acknowledgements

Cartoons in this book were previously published in the Insight section of *The Toronto Star*, under the title “Dusan’s World”.

I want to express my deep gratitude to the Insight editor Alfred Holden, whose sincere and enduring support is invisible, but a significant part of this book.

I also want to thank Kim McArthur, Kendra Martin, Devon Pool, Ann Ledden and Jelena Reljić for their enthusiasm and help with completing this book.

Dušan Petričić

Introduction

In 1993, when Dušan Petričić came to Toronto from Belgrade in what is now always called "the former Yugoslavia," he was generally seen as its leading political cartoonist. That is a charged and prestigious category in Europe, particularly eastern Europe, where political discussions during most of the twentieth century were coded rather than straightforward. This was especially true during the Soviet era when cartoonists, like playwrights, were significant figures; they had a limited licence to express dangerous thoughts. They were expected to both represent and defuse political passions. Dušan was viewed there as an artist, not a "mere" cartoonist, which is also part of the European tradition. One thinks immediately of Daumier, who painted, sculpted and made prints, alongside his indelible cartoons and caricatures. Dušan specialized, and still does, in exquisite illustrations of children's books. The time when he chose to move his work and his family to Canada coincided with the beginning of an ominous, and in many ways odious, decade in the Balkans.

He brought with him another European tendency as well, which you could call the intellectual style in drawing. In modern Europe, debates over ideas were often at the heart of political clashes, and editorial cartoonists never shied away from attempts to find pictorial equivalents for those complex ideas. They didn't simply focus on leaders and events. I think this conceptual element in Dušan's work resonates among Canadians. There's been a surprisingly intellectual cast to much of our cultural life, both in popular culture and the fine arts. I'm thinking for instance of Wayne and Shuster's success in comedy during almost fifty years on radio and TV. ("I'll have a martinus." "Do you mean a martini?" "If I want two, I'll ask for them.") Or Glenn Gould's music. Among the many versions of Bach's *Goldberg Variations*, Gould's is the one in which you can more or less hear him thinking as he plays. Canadian audiences seem comfortable with thoughts – which are essentially verbal in nature – being expressed in non-verbal forms.

I became aware of Dušan's status in the former Yugoslavia, and what he'd left behind to settle in Canada, when I visited Belgrade in 1995, in the midst of the vicious wars of disintegration there. I was speaking to a large gathering. The audience – largely writers, artists etc. – seemed anxious to prove (to me and/or themselves) that Serbia remained a highly cultured, civilized society, rather than a barbaric one, current evidence to the contrary. They were urgently concerned with connecting to writers and artists from elsewhere. When I finished my talk, the first question was: Can you tell us how Dušan is doing in Canada? That was five years after he'd left. They simply assumed any Canadian they encountered would know him, by his first name. It was a bit the way that Floridians might ask if you know their third cousin Jake who lives in Alberta, or maybe it's Montreal. I did happen to know Dušan; through sheer chance we'd been introduced by a Canadian political cartoonist on Bloor Street in Toronto. I assured them he was doing well. That may have disappointed them. I think they were hoping he'd return. He does continue to visit Belgrade regularly, and show his work there.

But for him now Toronto is clearly home, and he feels at home here, which is what you feel looking through this collection. He has an attachment to the place that many accomplished, cultivated, worldly immigrants also display. I confess I find a certain mystery in this widespread sense of connection. It sometimes amounts to an almost fervid protectiveness toward the city.

It isn't based on what typical homegrown boosters of the city, like the chamber of commerce, tourism bureau, local politicians or culture vultures often boast of. Certainly not on any of the "world class" features of Toronto – an embarrassing term betraying deep fears of inadequacy. Nor any of its highly touted restaurants (though some of the family-run ethnic eateries may be part of the appeal). Nor its extremely commercialized and otherwise undistinguished international film festival. If anything, such attractions are a net negative for sophisticated newcomers – except to the degree that they reveal an endearing vulnerability rooted in a sense of inferiority that reveals itself by trying too hard.

It seems to me what moves people like Dušan about Toronto is its high level of tolerance and acceptance for people from foreign backgrounds, and for the attitudes and other baggage that they bring with them. This usually falls under the heading of multiculturalism but if so, I think we are a special case of the genre. Canada is not alone in calling itself multicultural; it is now common in western societies. It accompanied the era of free trade and globalization. But elsewhere multiculturalism has been or become a contentious notion. The leaders of Germany, France and Britain have all recently declared it a failure. They want immigrants – in fact they can't do without them – but they'd like to dial back on the multiculturalism in the name of emphasizing and defending the fundamental of national culture. There is a clear element of electioneering and fearmongering in this retrenchment but it couldn't happen without a firm sense of what the "real" national character and traditions are: that which is truly French, truly German etc. That's what the "others" are expected to buy into.

The Canadian advantage may lie in the less defined nature of our national identity, and its brittleness. This is partly because Canada was constructed on a binational basis from its official beginning in 1867, and also because we have always lived in the shadow of imperial forces which were not just political and economic but cultural. This has created a cultural indistinctness and elasticity that can translate into accommodation. There isn't much here to form a backlash with. We may be more instinctively multicultural than those others because our own national culture is ill-defined and multiple already. That won't stop various people and parties, on both the left and right, from trying to rein in the multi quality of multiculturalism in the name of "Canadian" values; but those values are hard to pin down, even rhetorically, especially in a variegated population like Toronto's. The lack of solidity opens up a space for newcomers to make themselves at home as they are, rather than feeling pressured to make themselves over. What others often intuit when they arrive here is not a specific identity but a certain oblique yet welcoming openness, almost a curiosity – which itself seems to represent whatever is culturally unique about us. It's like a breathing space, so they relax and breathe.

The upshot isn't the reproduction of the old world and its cultures; that's hardly why someone like Dušan moves here. But it's a freedom to borrow freely from what they find and shape it on the basis of who they are and what they've brought along. So Dušan doesn't feel any need to pick from the official elements of Canadian identity as generations of immigrants to the U.S. tended to do. Think of the way, for instance, immigrant Jews to the U.S. went to Hollywood and carefully remade the official mythologies they found already existing: the western, the small town etc. There aren't any official elements here, or at least they're few – hockey, Tim Horton's – and what there is, is neither intimidating nor daunting. What's striking in Dušan's Toronto is the modesty of the themes and images that attract him: the Osborne Children's library or the fire halls on College Street and in the Beach. The old towers versus the new ones. The distances from one modest landmark to another.

You get to choose among many minor and local themes or images because nothing is major enough to impose itself. He glimpses his own version of Toronto through the screen of its self-importance, like the Torontonian he draws who's pulling back the curtain of the financial towers to get a glimpse of Lake Ontario, which Toronto seems to have mindlessly misplaced. Fortunately those towers for all their pomposity aren't that difficult to brush aside – they're as insubstantial for Dušan as our brief spring: an endearing moment between our freezing winters and our blistering summers. The absence of imposing cultural markers isn't a negative for immigrants like Dušan; it's the contrary, it's what gives them access and allows them to feel full membership in a very short time.

It's because the Canadian national sense of self is fragmented and regionalized, bilingual and multicultural – and still largely unformed – that a city like Toronto can welcome newcomers like Dušan and let them feel free to be themselves in both national and local senses. Almost nothing is compulsory, though good behaviour in the form of mutual tolerance is expected. This is not New York, that's the point. There is no Statue of Liberty lifting her lamp beside the golden door, illuminating the path and the myth that all newcomers are expected to adjust to, albeit in their own ways. There are instead a series of modest doors, like those he depicts in one of his most affectionate drawings, each opening into the next, letting you pass through Toronto at your own pace, according to your own light(s).

Rick Salutin

CITY OF NEWCOMERS

Київ
NEW DELHI
БЕОГРАД
DUŠAN

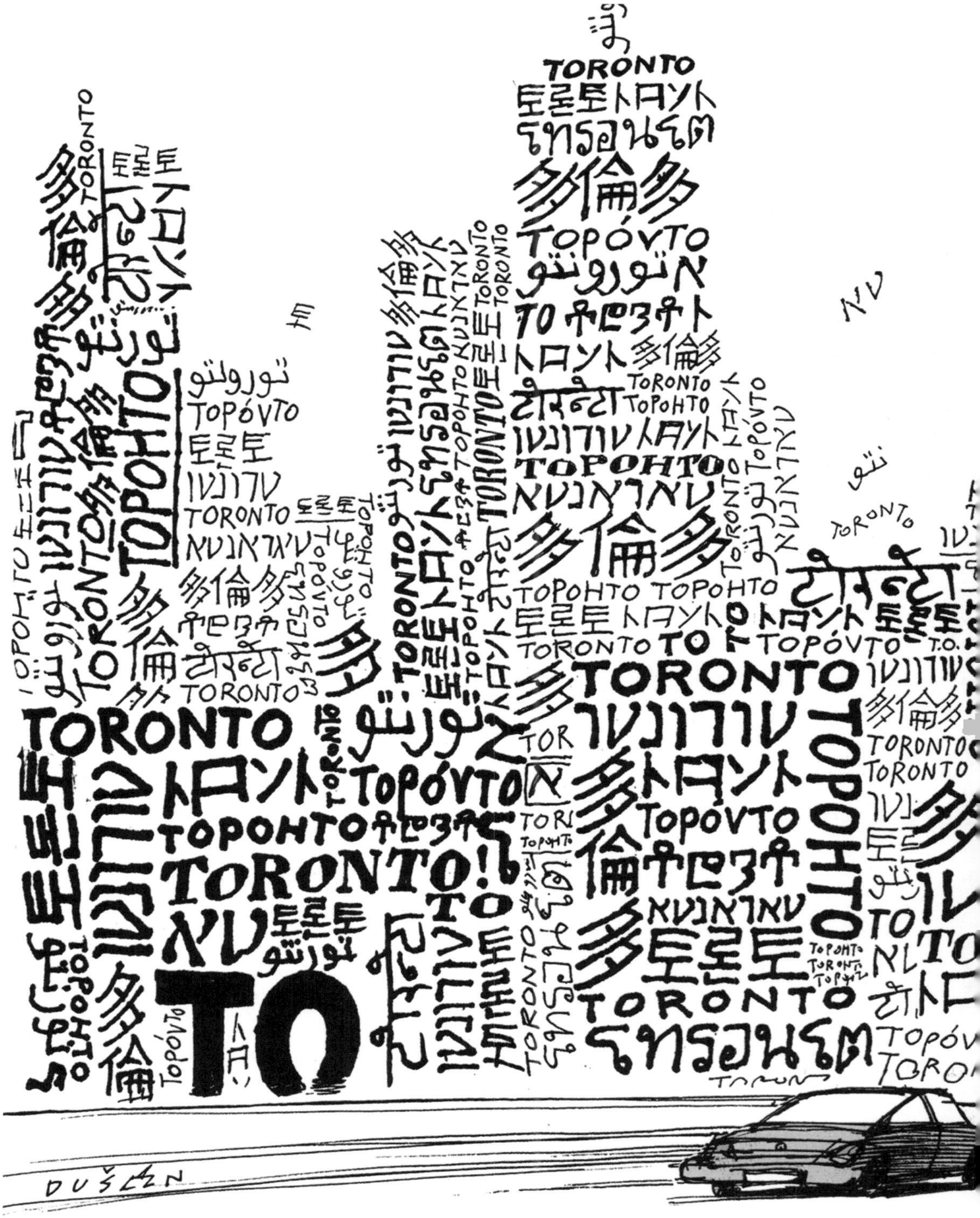
TORONTO
TOPOHTO
TOPÓVTO
TO
DUŠAN

TORONTO

JOB OPPORTUNITIES FOR NEWCOMERS

Lawyers
TAXI
Artists
TAXI
Teachers
DUŠAN

IMMIGRANT'S DREAM

EXCELLENT
JOB
HIGH SALARY
JOB
FOR YOU
JOB
IDEAL
JOB

TORONTO CLIMATE CONFUSIONS

DUŠAN

UARY - FEBRUARY

DUŠAN
ARCH-APRIL·MAY·JUNE-JULY-AUGUST-SE

FALL IN ONTARIO

WET
PAINT
DUŠAN

TORONTO
A (rainy) SUMMER 2008
COMBINATION

DUŠAN

CANADIAN WINTER SPECIES

WHITE SEAL

TORONTO WINTER BIKER

TORONTO MAP / WINTER '08

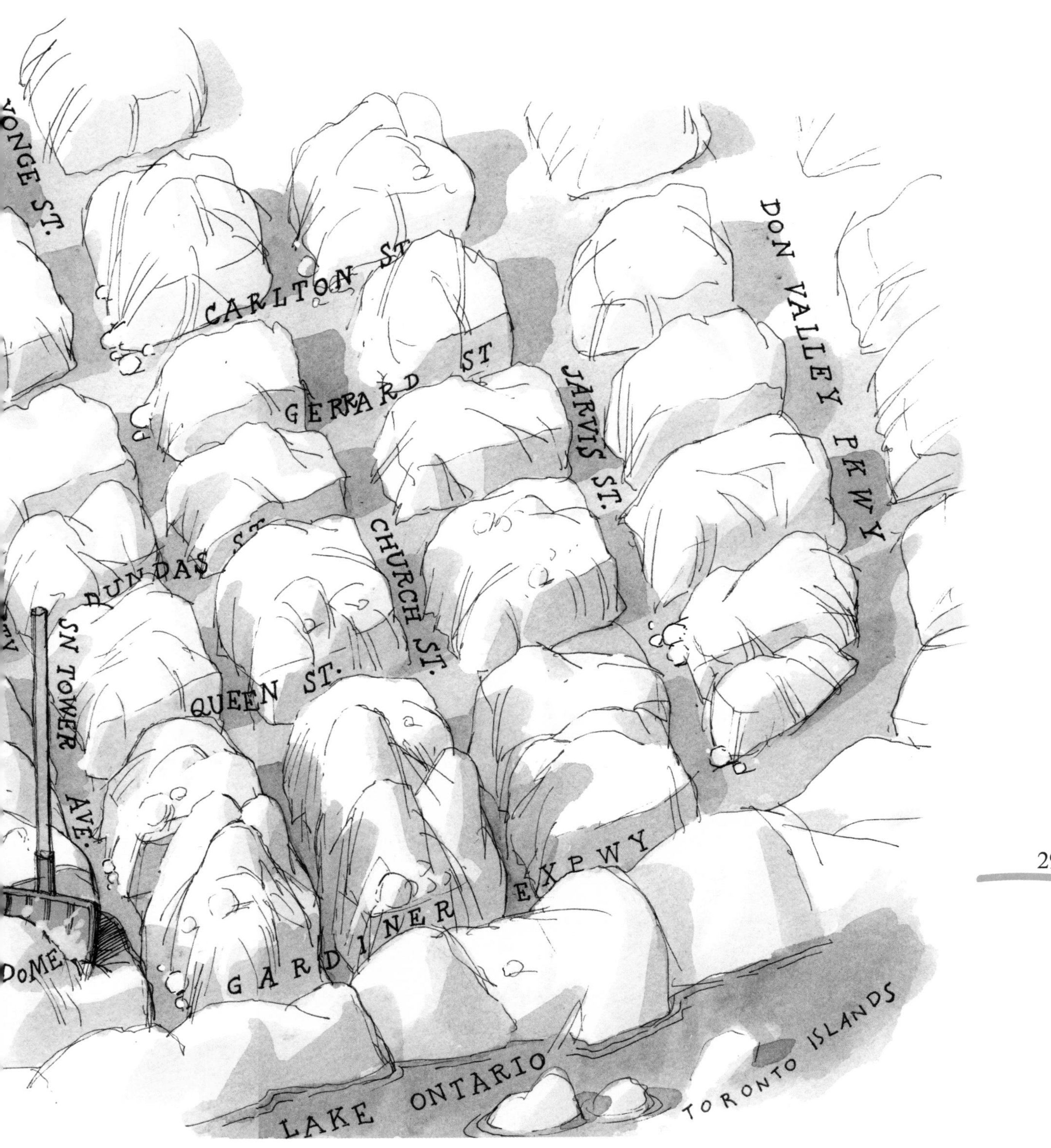

YONGE ST.
CARLTON ST
GERRARD ST
JARVIS ST.
DON VALLEY PKWY
DUNDAS ST
CHURCH ST.
QUEEN ST.
GARDINER EXPWY
LAKE ONTARIO
TORONTO ISLANDS

GREAT BUILDERS OF TORONTO

Ludvig Mies
van der Rohe
Viljo Revell
Peter Dickinson
Daniel Libeskind
I.M. Pei
Frank Gehry
John
Andrews
Raymond
Moriyama

Frank Gehry – *AGO*

Daniel
Libeskind
ROM

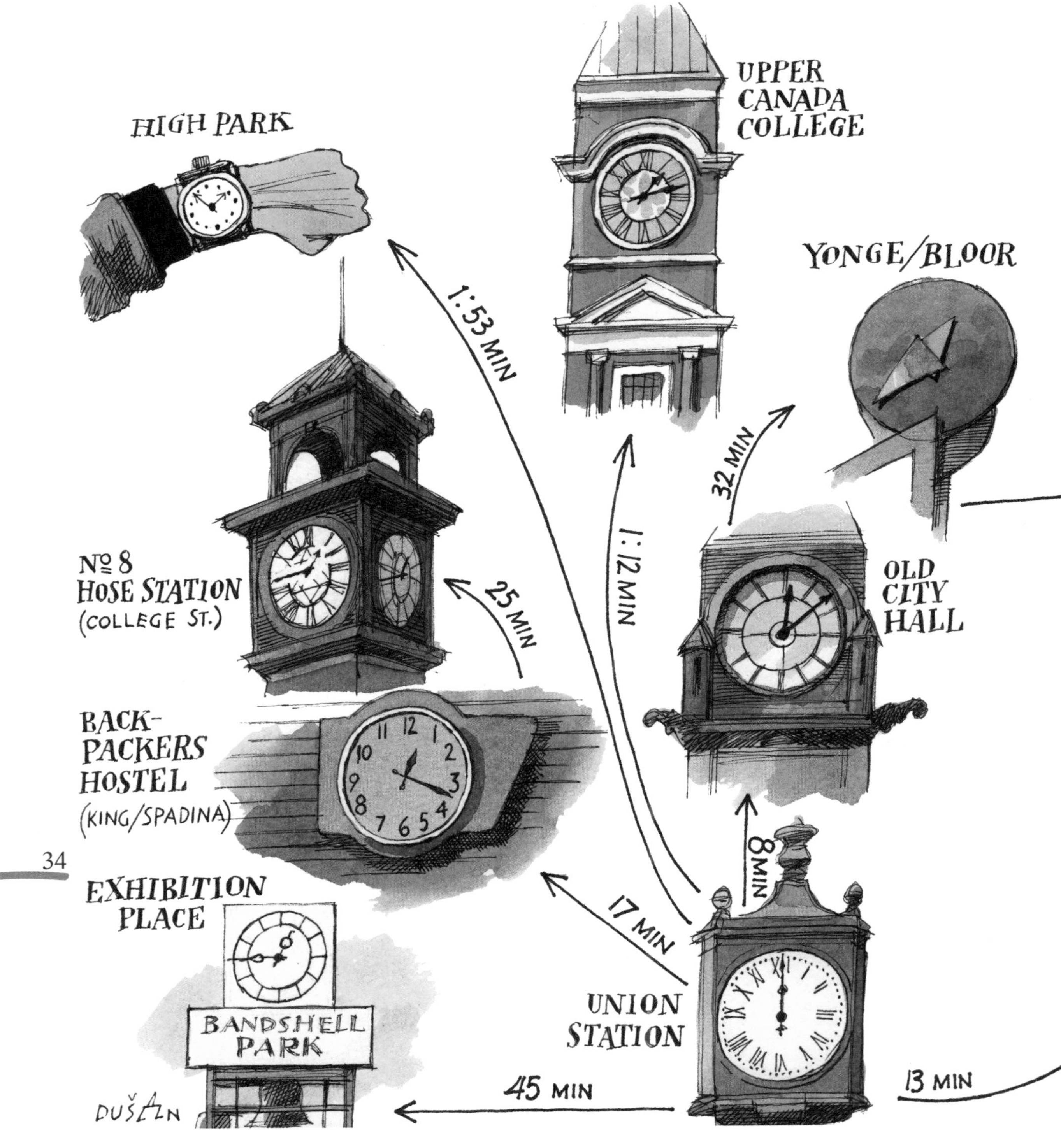

HIGH PARK
UPPER CANADA COLLEGE
YONGE/BLOOR
1:53 MIN
№ 8 HOSE STATION (COLLEGE ST.)
25 MIN
1:12 MIN
32 MIN
OLD CITY HALL
BACK-PACKERS HOSTEL (KING/SPADINA)
8 MIN
17 MIN
EXHIBITION PLACE
BANDSHELL PARK
UNION STATION
45 MIN
13 MIN
DUŠAN

HOW BIG IS TORONTO?

MEASURED BY WALKING DISTANCE

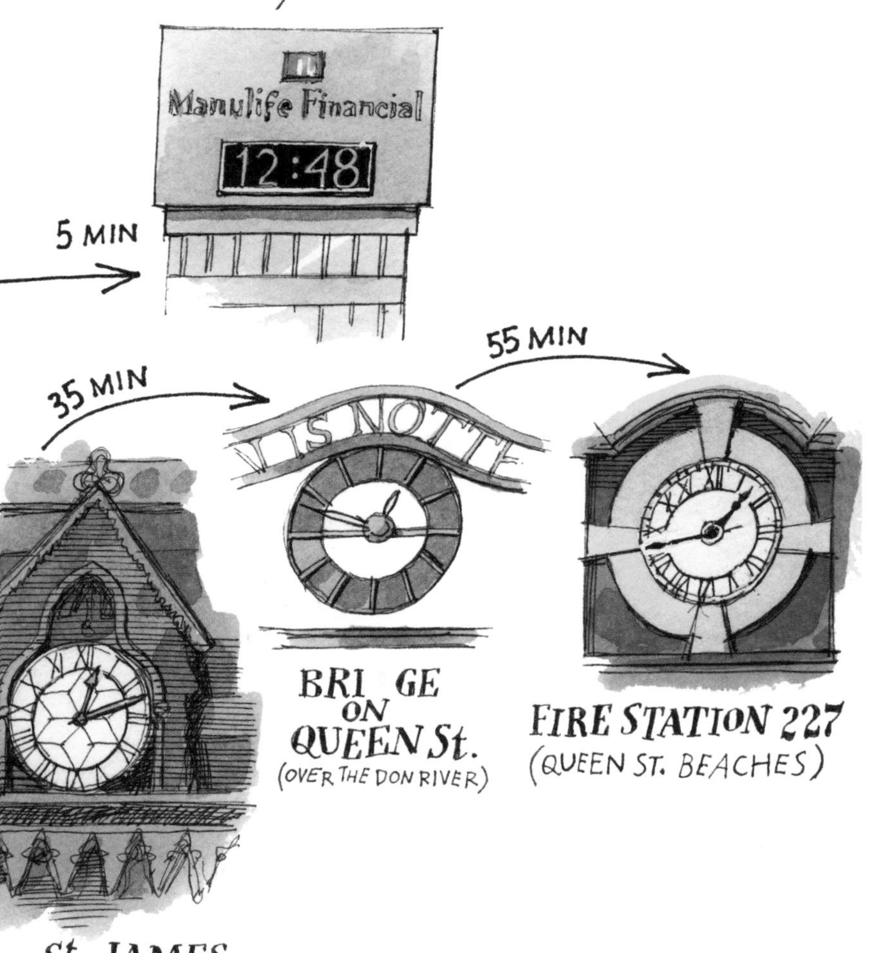

TORONTO'S SKYSCRAPERS

...AND NOW

NEW ROLE FOR SILOS

CANADA MALTING CO.
TORONTO
MUSEUM
DUŠAN

HOW TO MAKE GARDINER LOVEABLE

501 QUEEN STREETCAR

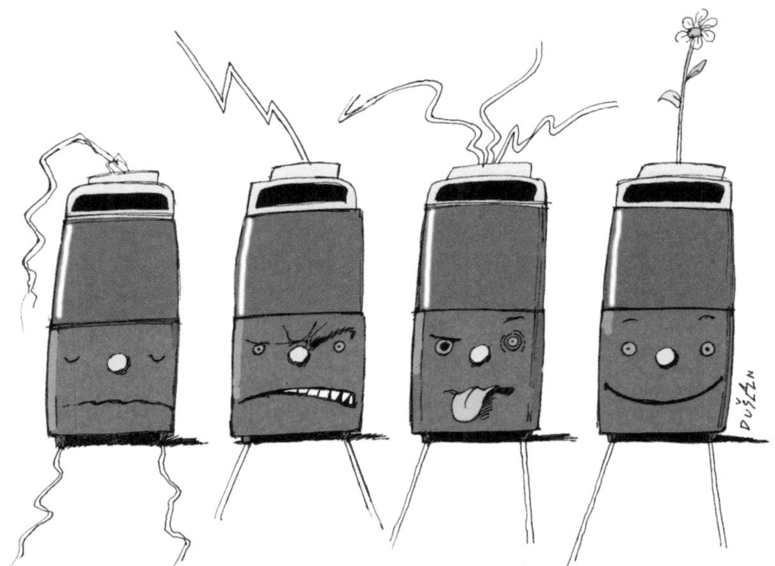
DUŠAN

LONG BRANCH

BRIDGES OF TORONTO

THERE ARE 500 BRIDGES OF DIFFERENT KINDS AND SHAPES

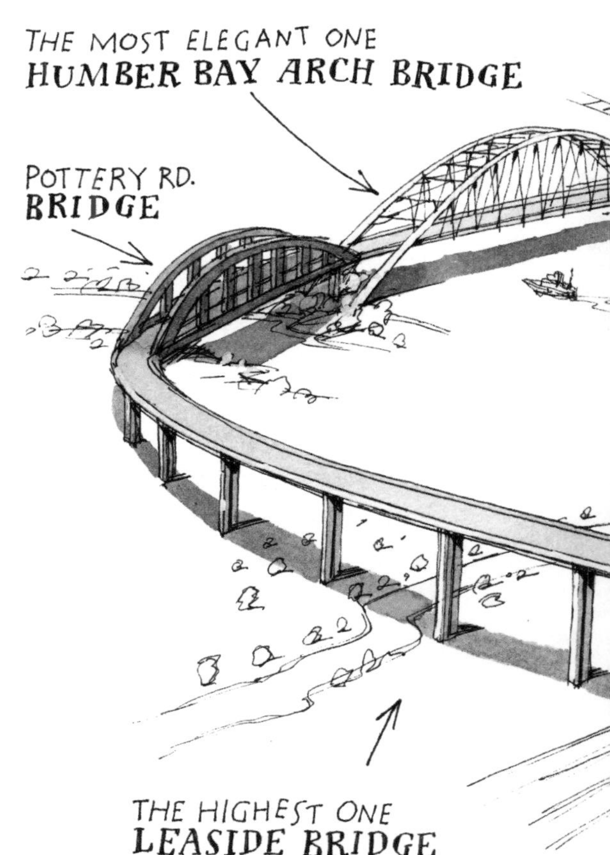

NON-EXISTING ONE
ISLAND AIRPORT
BRIDGE

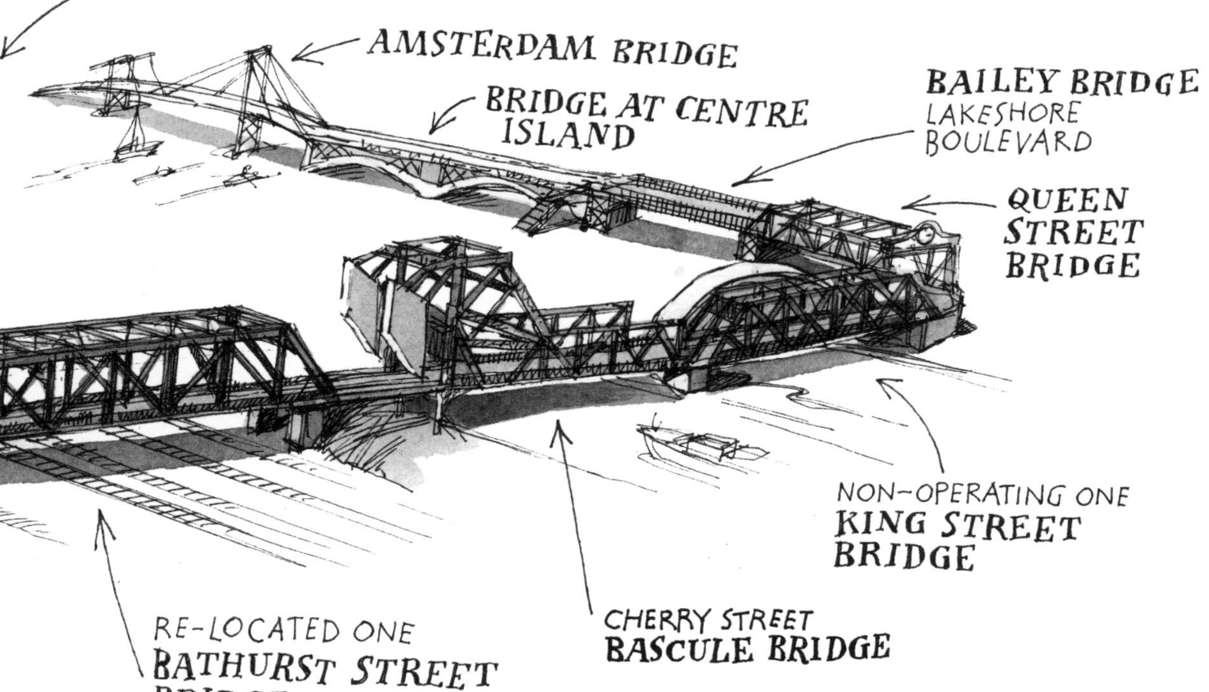
AMSTERDAM BRIDGE
BRIDGE AT CENTRE
ISLAND
BAILEY BRIDGE
LAKESHORE
BOULEVARD
QUEEN
STREET
BRIDGE
NON-OPERATING ONE
KING STREET
BRIDGE
RE-LOCATED ONE
BATHURST STREET
BRIDGE
CHERRY STREET
BASCULE BRIDGE

THE MOST FAMOUS ONE
PRINCE EDWARD VIADUCT

TORONTO DISTILLERY

1832

2010

Native Canadian Centre of Toronto
George Brown House
Campbell House
LCBO North Toronto Station
Hare Krishna Temple
10
DUŠCZN

etc
St. Paul's Basilica
Elgin and Winter Garden Theatre
Church of the Holy Trinity
Arts & Letters Club of Toronto
Heliconian Hall

OSBORNE COLLECTION

SWEET ARCHITECTURE

07
2000

YORKVILLE – The Times, They Are A-changin'

BOB DYLAN

TORONTO / LAKE VIEW

DUŠAN 2007

'TIS THE SEASON AT VAUGHAN MILLS

CHINA
PACIFIC
CANADA
DUŠAN

PACIFIC MALL

DUŠAN

CITY PLANNING

MODERN CONDO LIVING

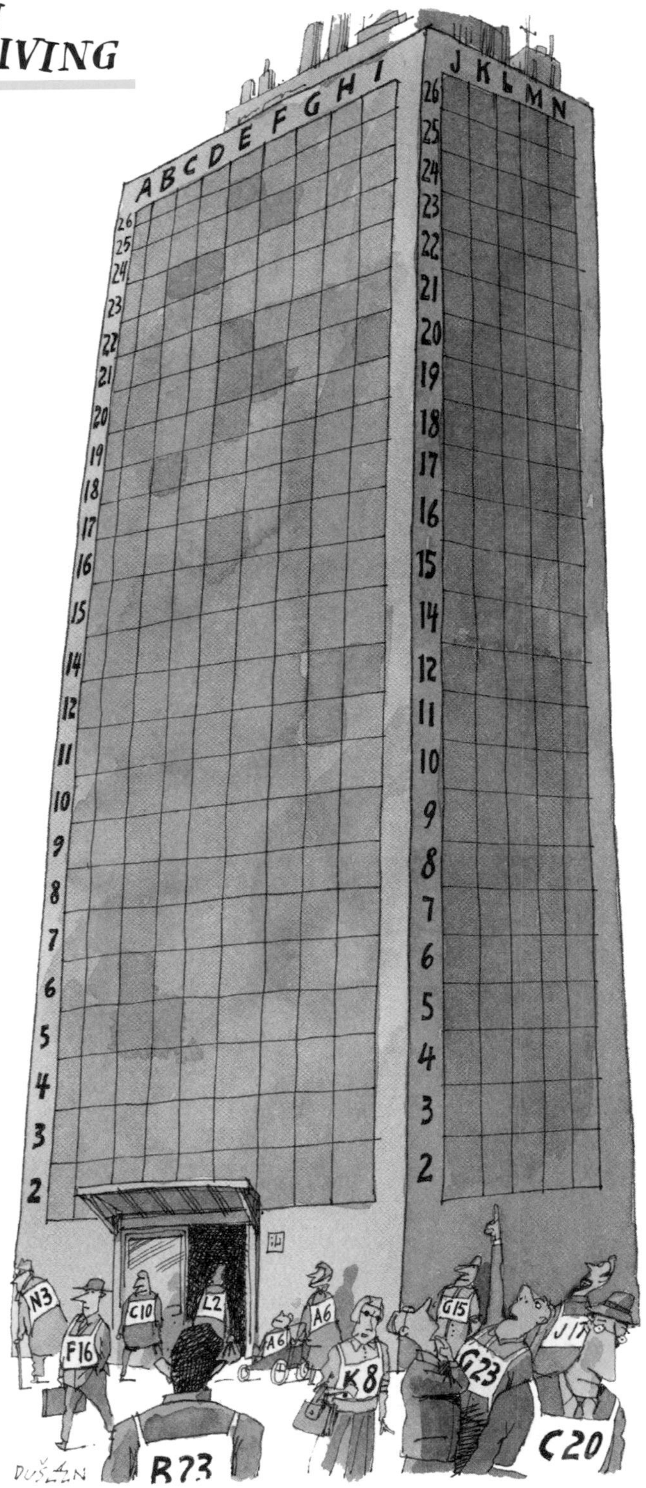

FAÇADISM

DOWNTOWN CONDO

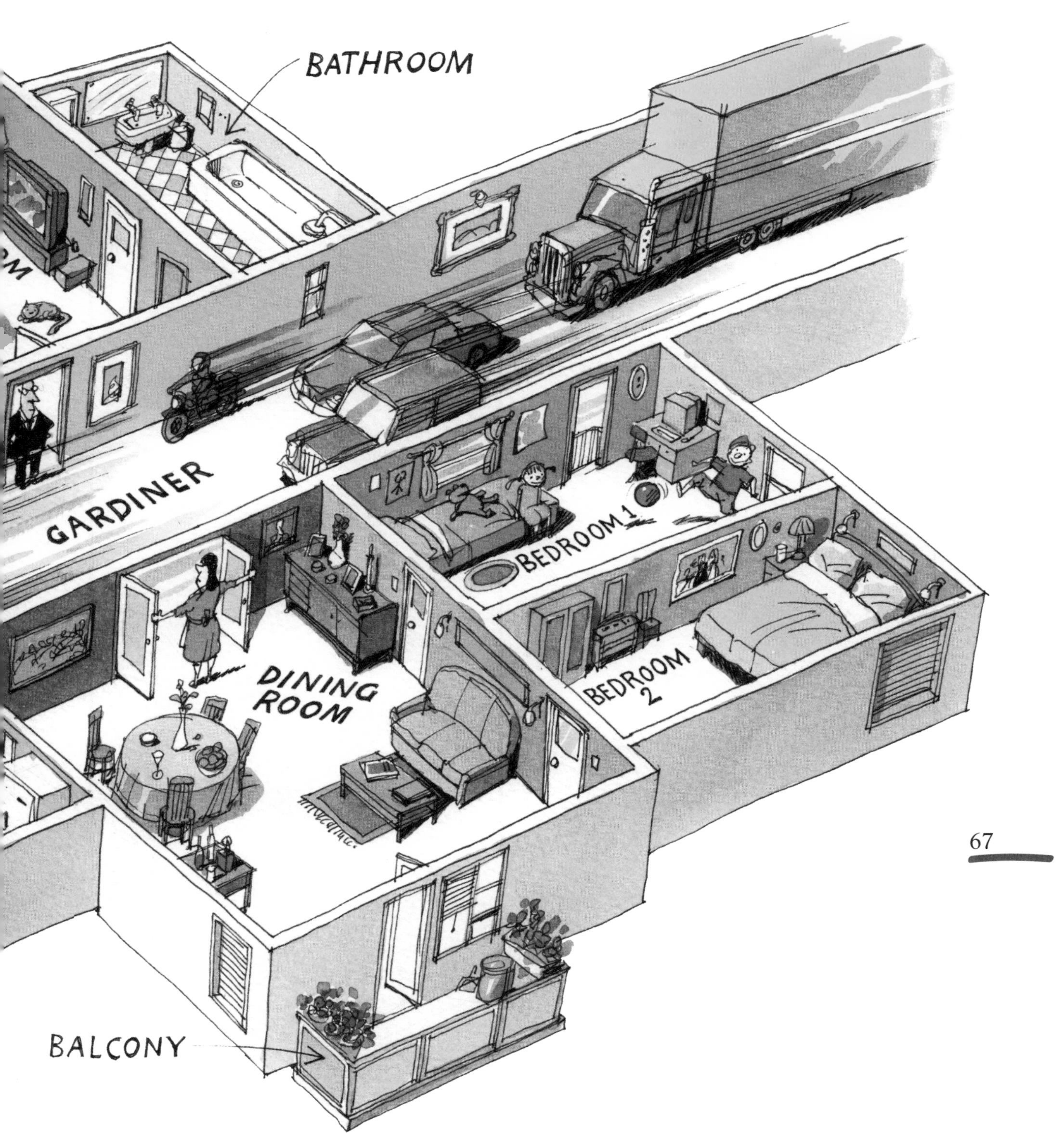
BATHROOM
GARDINER
BEDROOM 1
BEDROOM 2
DINING ROOM
BALCONY

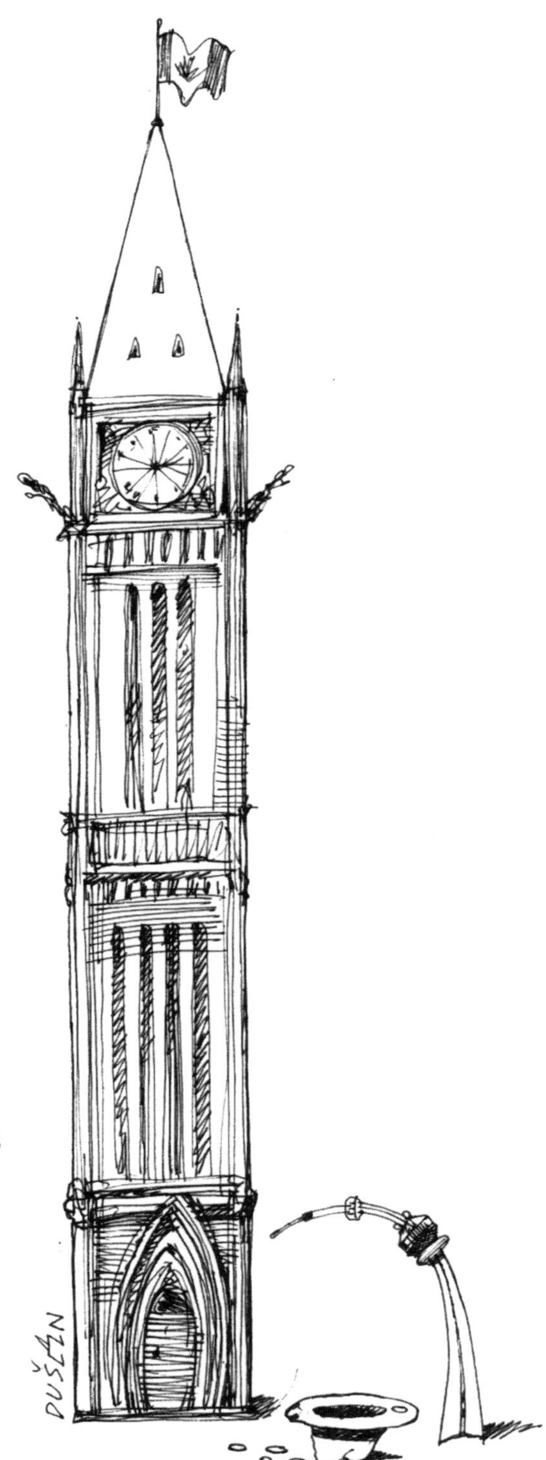
DUŠAN

TORONTO REFLECTIONS

NEW IN TOWN

SUGAR BEACH

TORONTO ZOO

LANDED IMMIGRANTS
DUŠAN

DON RIVER ENVIRONMENT

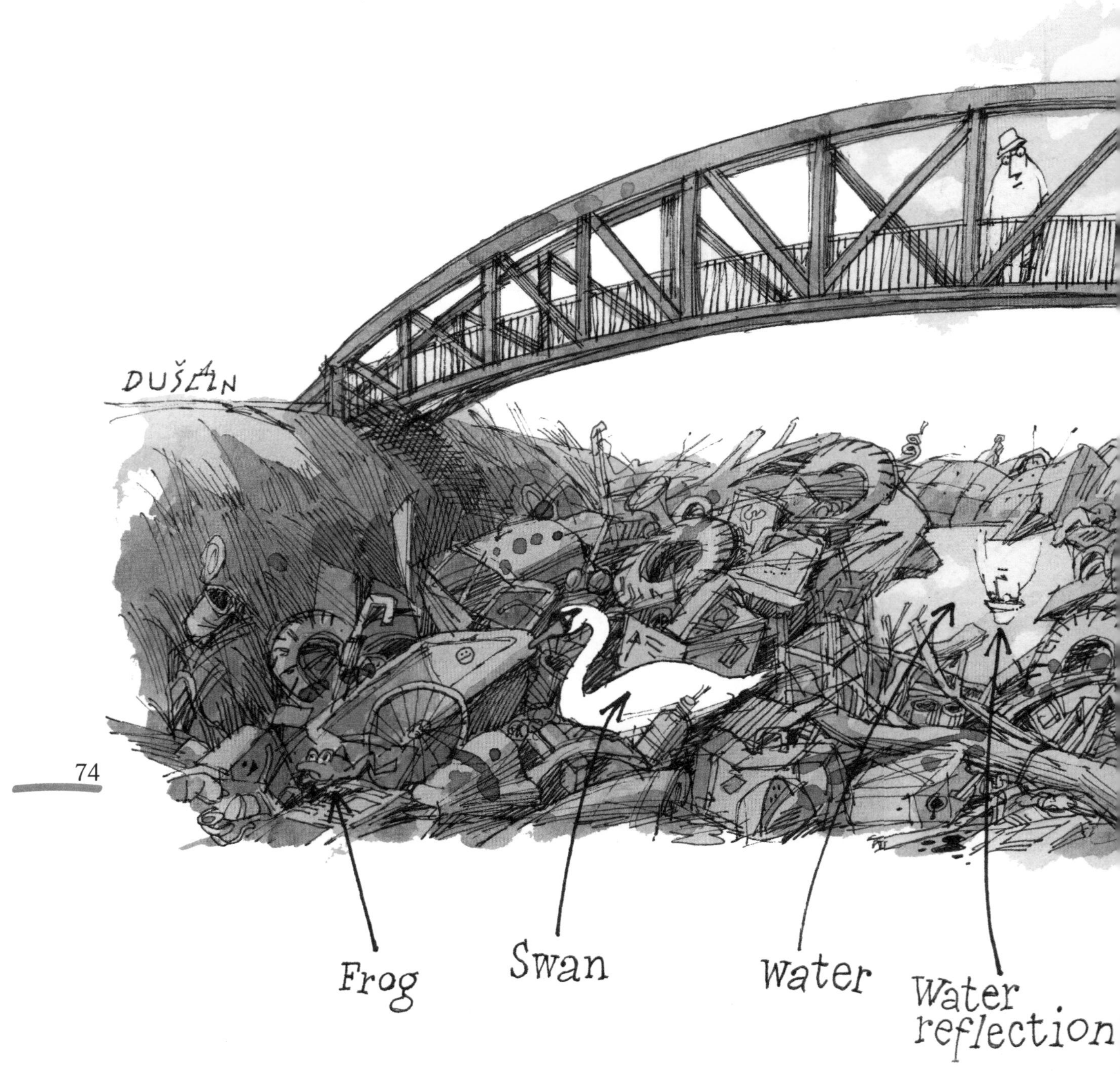

Fish

Water

Ducks

Fish

Flora

The NATIONAL GALLERY
OTTAWA
The 1930s: The NEW MAN
6 JUNE
MUSEUM OF
FINE ARTS
MONTREAL
YVES SAINT LAURENT
ART SCENE IN
TORONTO

76

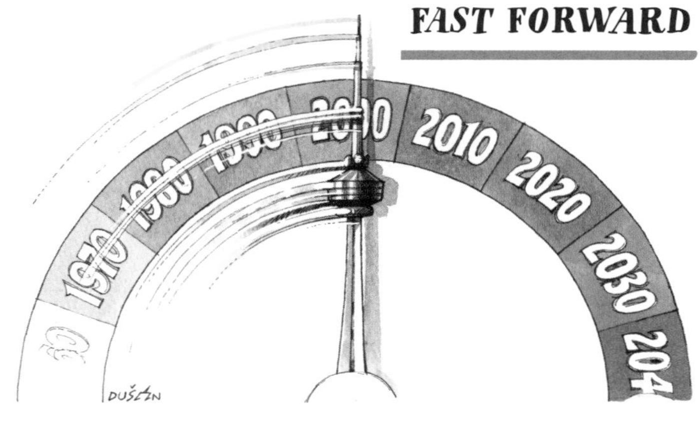
FAST FORWARD
1970
2010
2020
2030

TAIPEI,
KUALA LUMPUR,
CHICAGO,
SHANGHAI,
HONG KONG...

...DUBAI
TORONTO STAR 07

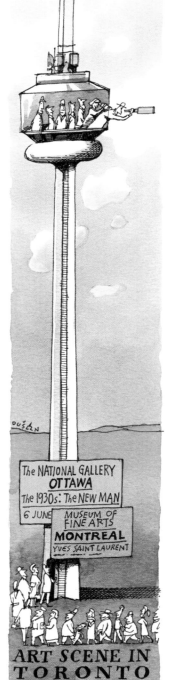

DUSAN

TIFF
BEN KINGSLEY
JEREMY IRONS
ADRIEN BRODY
CHARLIZE THERON
MATT DAMON
BRAD PITT
JULIANNE MOORE
BENICIO DEL TORO
DUŠAN

CARIBANA

Anguilla
St. Maarten
Antigua
Montserrat
Toronto
Guadalupe
Dominica
Martinique
St. Lucia
St. Vincent
Barbados
Grenada
Tobago
Trinidad
DUŠAN

Menu

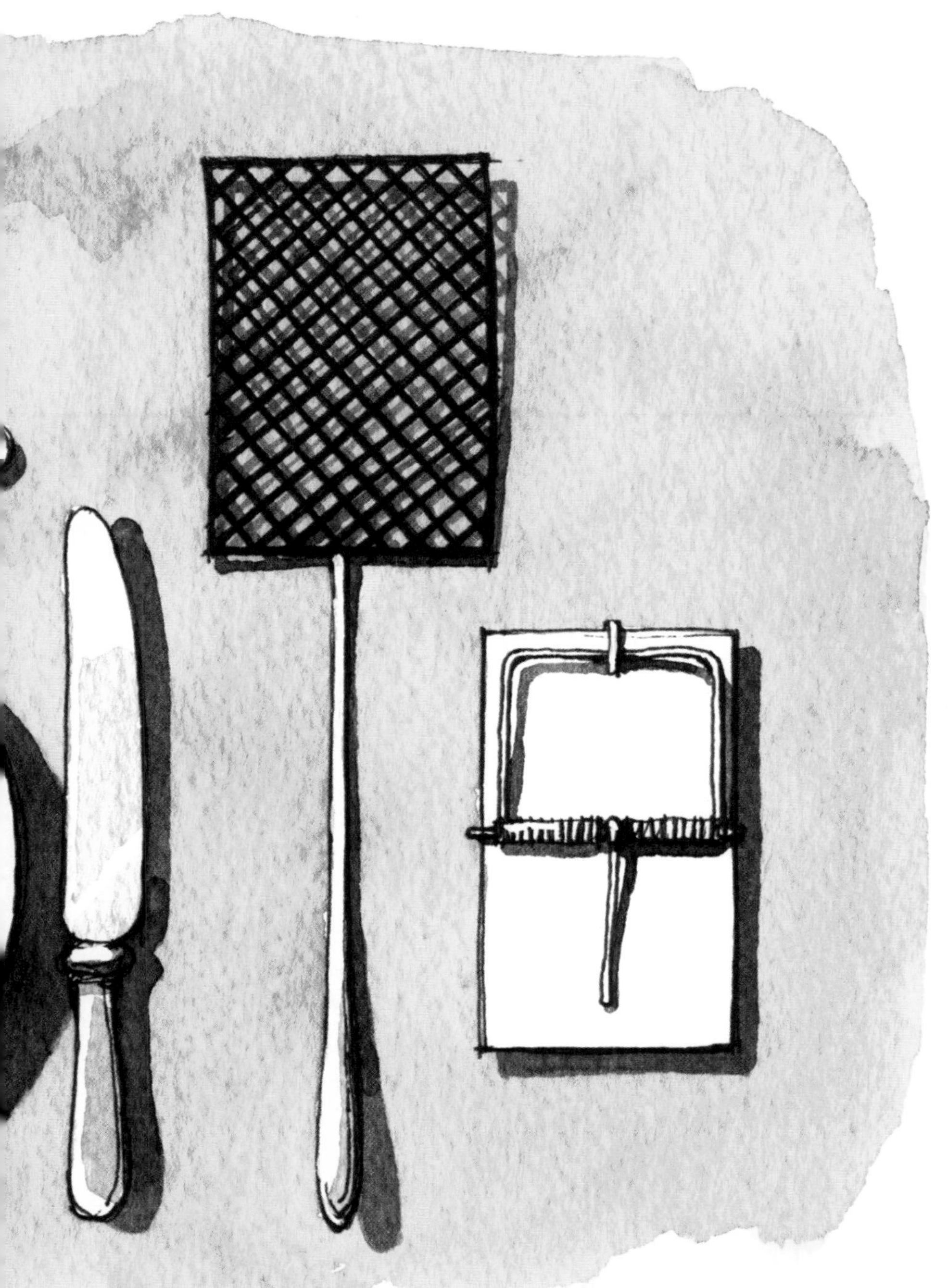

ROM

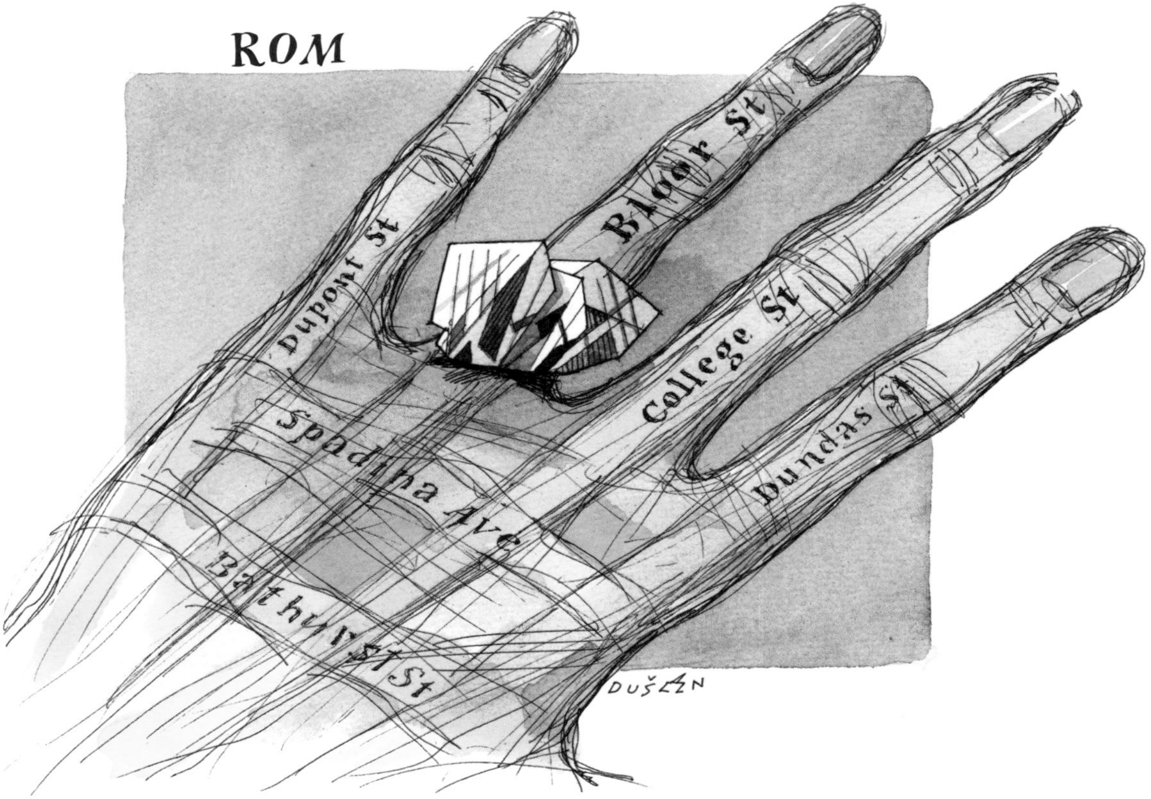

INTERNET ERA

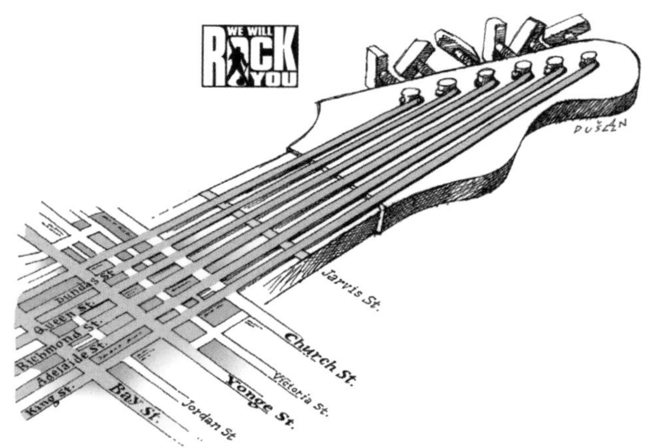

WORD ON THE STREET

KEEP YOUR EYES ON THE ROAD
DRIVE NOW READ LATER.
DON'T LOOK HERE!
DON'T GET DISTRACTED
FOCUS ON DRIVING!
DUŠAN

PROPOSAL FOR A MORE APPROPRIATE HIGHWAY BILLBOARD MESSAGES

TORONTO'S FAVOURITE GAME

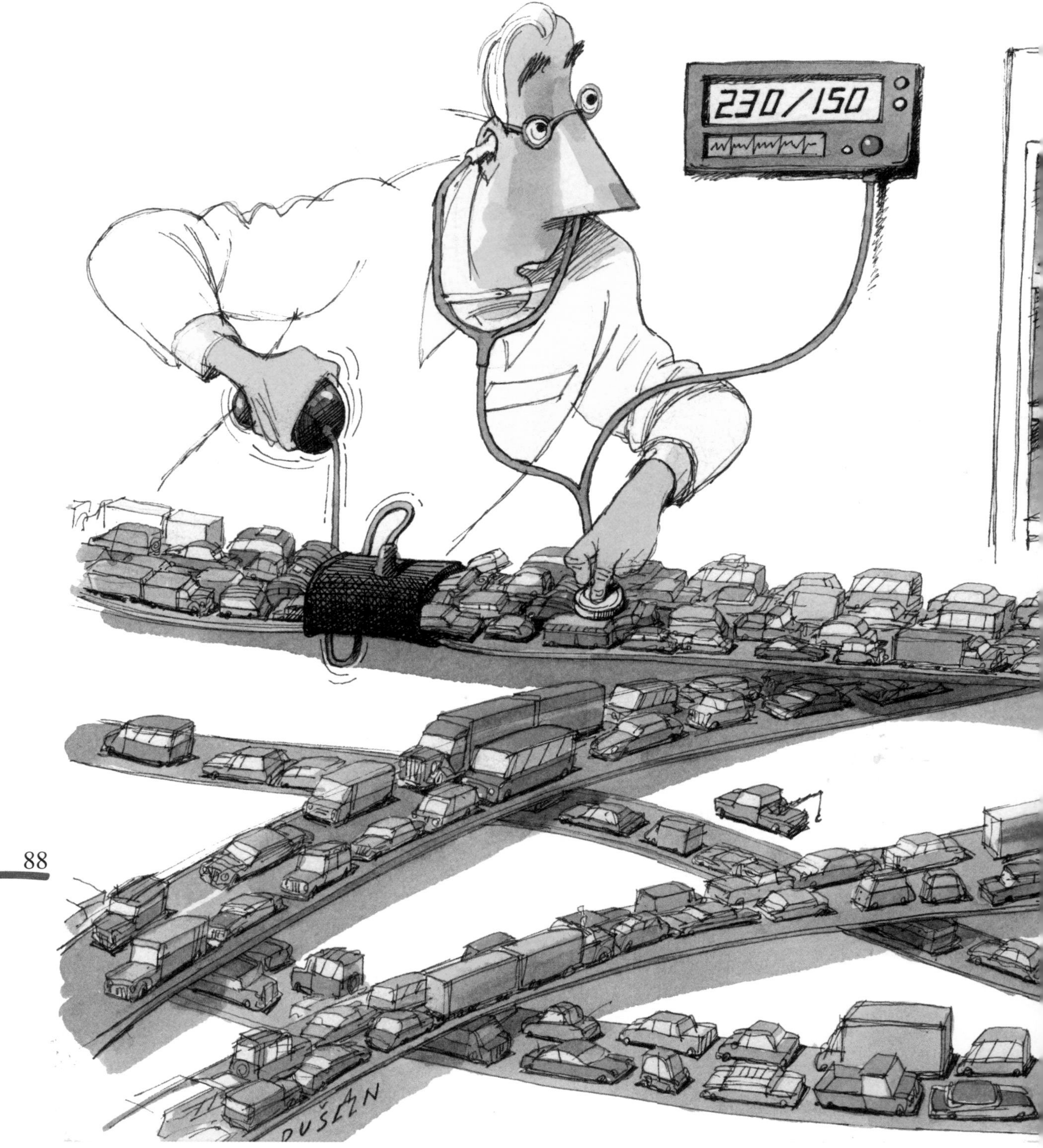
230/150

GTA TRAFFIC

BATTLE FOR THE STREETS

Lawrence Ave. W.
Eglinton Ave. W.
Avenue Rd.
St. Clair Ave. W.
Spadina Ave.
Bloor St. W.
Yonge St.
College St.
Bay St.
University Ave.
Dundas St. W.
Queen St. W.
King St. W.

Lawrence Ave. E.
Eglinton Ave. E.
Mt. Pleasant Rd.
St. Clair Ave. E.
DUŠAN
loor St. E.
Danforth
DON VALLEY PKWY
Jarvis St.
ton St.
Dundas St. E.
Church St.
Queen St. E.
King St. E.

THE HOTTEST CAR OF THE SEASON

DUŠAN

DOUBLE ROLE

PRACTICAL PROPOSAL FOR SMOKERS

TORONTO GARAGES

DUŠAN

LONG WEEKEND

DUŠAN

TORONTONIANS

High Park
Conifer
Black Oak
Grass
DUŠAN

Sugar Maple
Jemima Howard
Grenadier Pond
Dog Hill

SLEEPING BEAUTIES (1)

OLD BRIDGE OVER DON RIVER (EASTERN AVE.)

QUIRKY SUGGESTIONS FOR SOME
OF TORONTO'S FORGOTTEN STRUCTURES

SLEEPING BEAUTIES (2)
OLD DOWNSVIEW HANGARS
QUIRKY SUGGESTIONS FOR SOME
OF TORONTO'S FORGOTTEN STRUCTURES

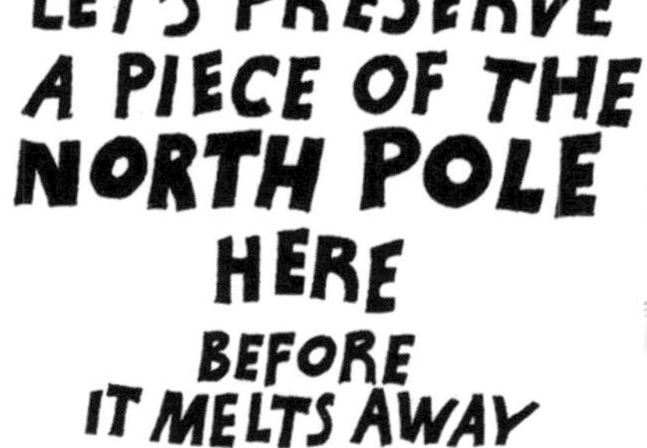
LET'S PRESERVE
A PIECE OF THE
NORTH POLE
HERE
BEFORE
IT MELTS AWAY

NORTH POLE

DUŠAN

TWO NEW PROPOSALS FOR THE GARDINER

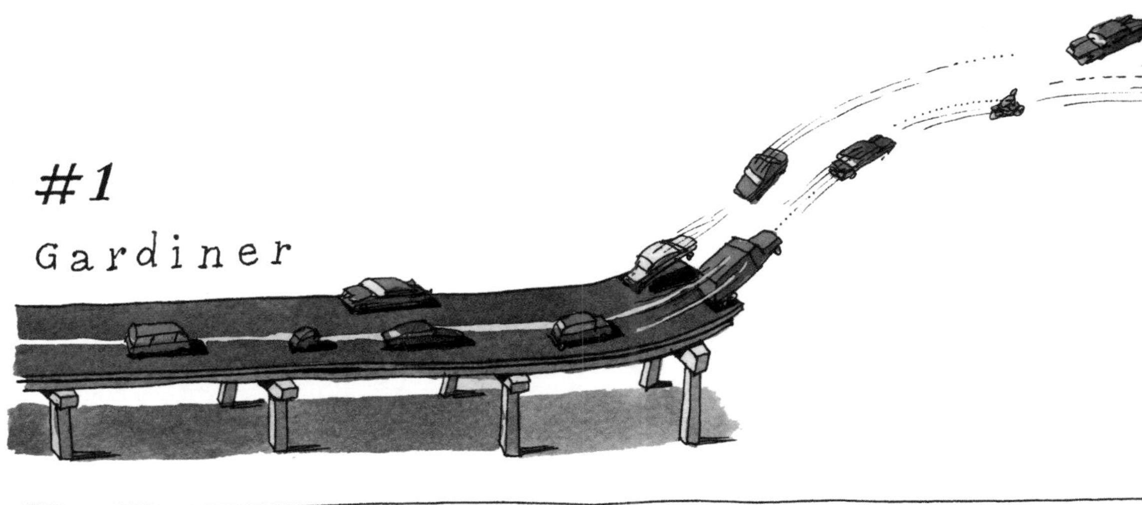

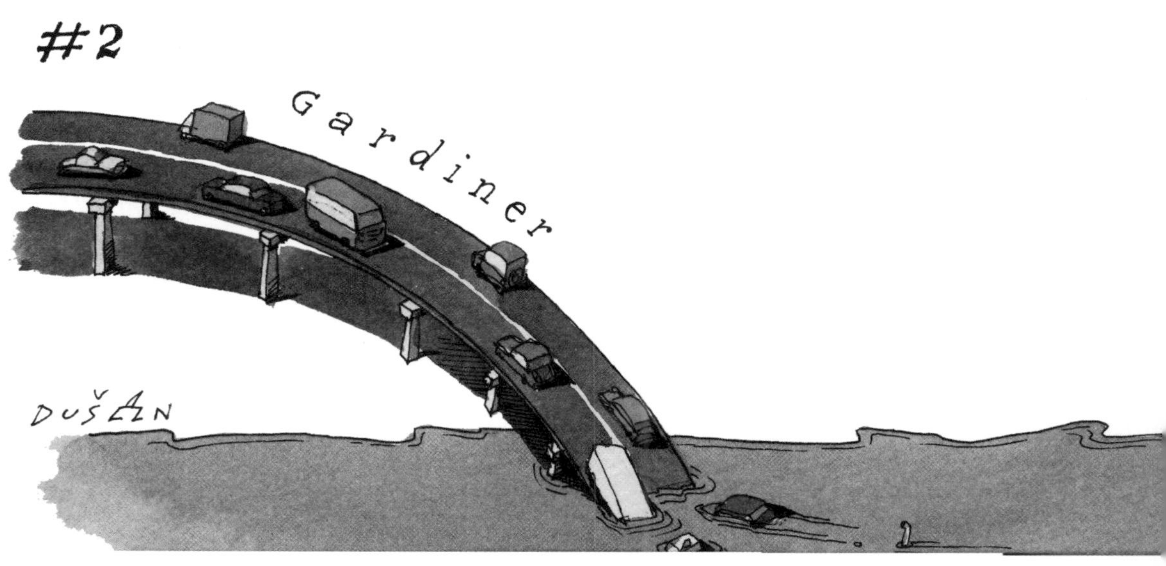

Don Valley Pkwy

Don Valley Pkwy

416 and 905

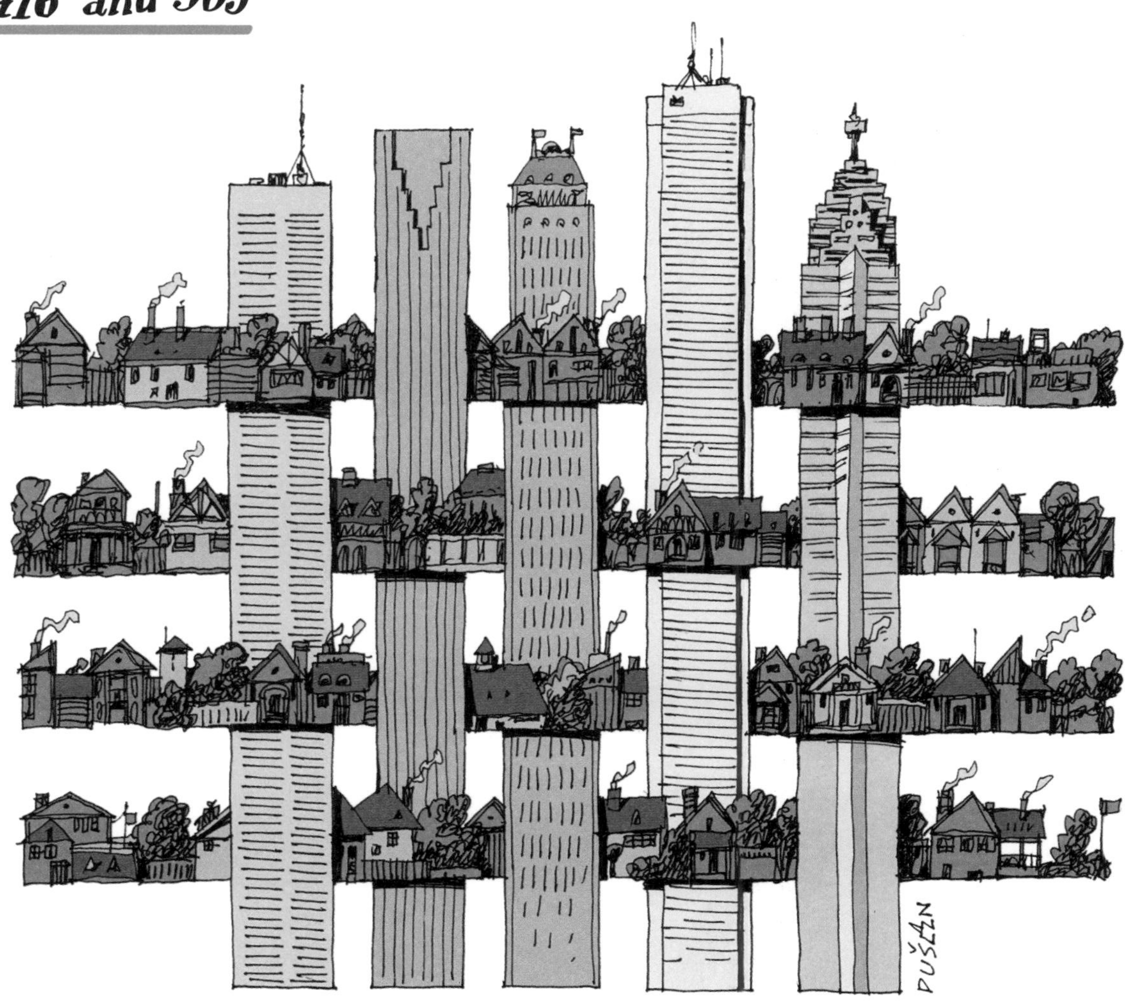